Making Pictures
SPOOKY THINGS

Materials

Start collecting materials to make the wonderful pictures in this book. You'll need paper and poster board, yarn and felt, sequins and beads, foil, glitter and paints, sponges, and fancy candy wrappers.

You can either make the pictures just the same as the ones in the book, or you can use the ideas to design your own. There are all sorts of exciting and unusual painting techniques for you to try out, too.

Designed by **Jane Warring**
Illustrations by **Lindy Norton**
Pictures made by **Karen Radford**
Photographs by **Peter Millard**

This edition © 1997 Thumbprint Books
Published by Rigby Interactive Library,
an imprint of Rigby Education
a division of Reed Elsevier, Inc.
500 Coventry Lane, Crystal Lake, IL 60014

Printed in Italy

00 99 98 97 96
10 9 8 7 6 5 4 3 2 1

Library of Congress Cataloging-in-Publication Data

King, Penny, 1963-
   Spooky things / Penny King and Clare Roundhill.
      p.   cm. -- (Making pictures)
   Includes index.
   Summary: Gives directions for creating collages of witches,
monsters, and other spooky things.
      ISBN 1-57572-195-3 (lib.bdg.)
   1. Collage--Juvenile literature. 2. Halloween decorations-
-Juvenile literature. (1. Collage. 2. Halloween decorations.
3. Handicraft.) I. Roundhill, Clare, 1964-   . II. Title.
III. Series: King, Penny 1963- Making pictures.
TT910-K567 1997
702'.8'12--DC21

                                                    96-40518
                                                       CIP
                                                        AC

Making Pictures
SPOOKY THINGS

Penny King and Clare Roundhill

Contents

Grinning Ghosts

Create this picture of a family of ghosts gliding across a starry sky. Add extra special stars made from yellow poster board glued onto tiny pieces of sponge. Decorate the ghosts with sparkling red eyes, grinning mouths, and silver glitter.

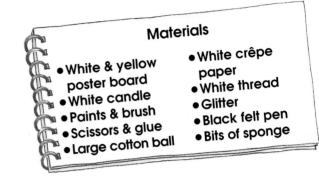

Materials

- White & yellow poster board
- White candle
- Paints & brush
- Scissors & glue
- Large cotton ball
- White crêpe paper
- White thread
- Glitter
- Black felt pen
- Bits of sponge

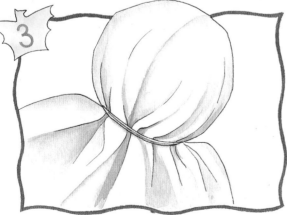

Draw little stars all over the white board, using the end of the candle. Press down hard.

Paint over the stars with watery dark blue paint (see paint tip). Let the paint dry.

Put a large cotton ball in the center of a white crêpe square. Tie it in place with white thread.

Add red glitter eyes, black mouths, and silver glitter to each ghost. Glue them on the sky.

A Haunted Wood

Create a creepy crêpe haunted wood swarming with spooky creatures.

Give it a misty, eerie look by gluing thin wisps of cotton over the trees.

Paint a misty background on a long piece of poster board or stiff paper (see paint tip).

Cut thick tree trunks from black crêpe paper with the wrinkles going from top to bottom.

Materials

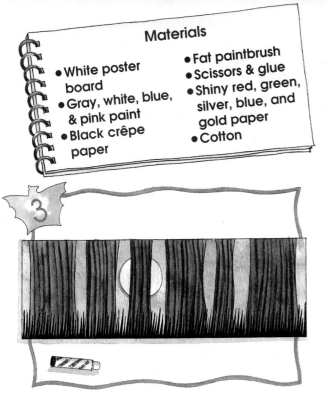

- White poster board
- Gray, white, blue, & pink paint
- Black crêpe paper
- Fat paintbrush
- Scissors & glue
- Shiny red, green, silver, blue, and gold paper
- Cotton

PAINT TIP
Brush water all over the piece of white poster board until it is quite wet. Using a fat brush, paint thick streaks of pale gray, blue, and pink across the paper. Let it dry.

3

Glue a big silver moon and the wrinkly tree trunks onto the sky. Add spiky crêpe paper grass.

4

Cut spooky eyes out of shiny paper. Glue them on the trees. Add a layer of cotton mist.

9

A Mad Monster

Let your imagination go wild when you make this mad monster picture. Give it eyes that stick out on stalks, big ears, a spotty nose, and a huge tongue. Make a mad pipe cleaner spider with beady eyes to stick in its hideous hair.

Materials

- Lid of a box
- Paints & brush
- Sponges
- Scissors & glue
- Black & red poster board
- Red felt
- 2 corks
- Silver foil
- Black yarn
- Pipe cleaners
- 2 small beads

1 Paint the lid (see paint tip). Cut out sponge ears, a tongue, and nose. Paint spots on the nose.

2 Glue red felt eyes onto circles of black board. Glue the eyes onto two pieces of sponge.

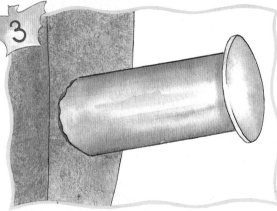

3 Cover two corks with foil. Glue foil circles on top. Cut holes in the lid and push in the corks.

4 Glue the eyes, ears, tongue, nose, and yarn hair onto the head. Glue it on red board.

PAINT TIP

Make different shades of green using blue, yellow, and green paint. Dab the paint all over the box lid with a piece of sponge. Overlap the shades while the paint is wet to give a blotchy effect.

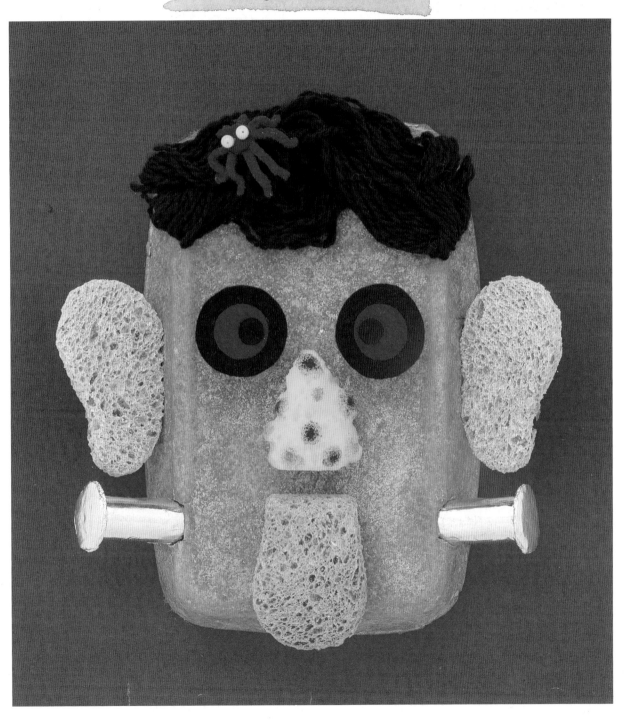

A Scaredy Cat

This cat is frightened of the streaks of lightning flashing across the sky. Look how her back arches and her hair stands on end! Make the lightning really glow by spreading zigzags of glue on the board. Then sprinkle them with glitter.

Materials
- Stiff white paper
- Scissors & glue
- Black, gray, and white paint
- Paintbrush
- Shiny paper
- Silver & gold glitter
- Green poster board
- Black pipe cleaners

Draw the outline of a cat with an arched back and upright tail on white paper. Cut it out.

Paint the cat with zigzags of black, gray, and white paint mixed with glue (see paint tip).

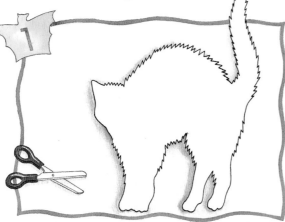

Before the paint dries, sprinkle glitter all over the cat. Glue the cat onto the green board.

Paint a nose and mouth. Glue on pipe cleaner whiskers, paper eyes, and claws. Add lightning.

PAINT TIP
For the cat's stripes, mix an
equal amount of black paint
with some glue. Do the
same with some gray and
white paint. The glue makes
the glitter stick to the
wet paint.

13

A Mysterious Mirror

In this picture, a ghostly creature appears to loom out of an ancient mirror, hanging above a hot, roaring fire. To make the creature look mysterious, give it red eyes that glow in the dark, and long, claw-like silver fingers.

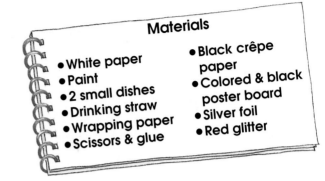

Materials
- White paper
- Paint
- 2 small dishes
- Drinking straw
- Wrapping paper
- Scissors & glue
- Black crêpe paper
- Colored & black poster board
- Silver foil
- Red glitter

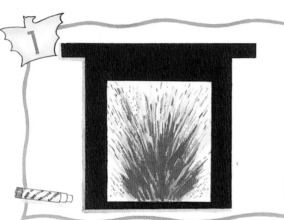

1. Paint a fire on white paper (see paint tip). Glue it onto a black poster board fireplace.

2. Glue the fireplace onto the wrapping paper. Glue on crumpled black crêpe coal.

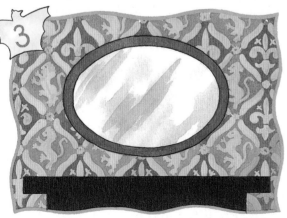

3. Glue a brown poster board oval to the wrapping paper. Glue a silver oval on top.

4. Mold a foil face and hands. Glue them on the mirror. Add poster board candlesticks.

PAINT TIP
Put red and yellow paint in two separate dishes. Suck up half a straw of red paint. Blow and spatter it over the white paper. Do the same with yellow paint. Repeat this to make a roaring fire. Be careful not to swallow it!

15

A Moaning Mummy

Make this ghostly picture of a mummy slowly rising from its deep, dark tomb.

Give it large, sunken black eyes with big, silver glitter pupils, and a sad mouth.

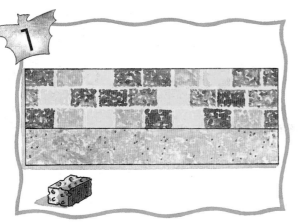

Sponge a brick pattern onto yellow board (see paint tip). Glue brown rice underneath.

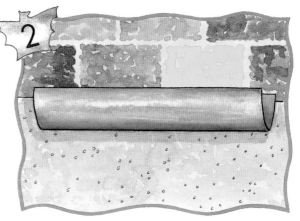

Cut the cardboard tube in half along its length. Cover it in silver foil. Stick it on the brown rice.

PAINT TIP
Cut a small rectangle out of a sponge. Soak it in water and then squeeze it dry. Press it in orange paint. Print rows of bricks along the top half of the yellow poster board, leaving a space between each one. Let the paint dry before you glue the brown rice on the bottom half.

16

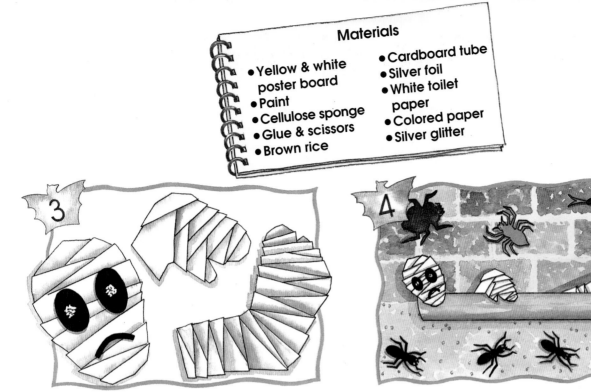

Materials

- Yellow & white poster board
- Paint
- Cellulose sponge
- Glue & scissors
- Brown rice
- Cardboard tube
- Silver foil
- White toilet paper
- Colored paper
- Silver glitter

3

Cut out a board head, hand, and foot. Wrap them in toilet paper. Add a mouth and eyes.

4

Glue the mummy onto the tomb. Glue colored paper creepy crawlies all around it.

A Shocking Skeleton

You'll need different kinds and shapes of pasta to make this smiling, shaking skeleton. If you want to make him extra spooky, paint the pasta with fluorescent colors before you stick them down, so that he glows in the dark.

Materials

- Black poster board
- Different kinds of pasta - thick & thin macaroni, twirls, & bows
- White crayon
- Glue & knife
- Popping corn
- Big potato
- White paint
- Old plate

Draw a skeleton in crayon on black poster board. Choose pasta shapes for all the bones.

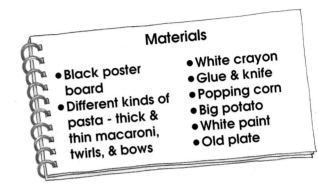

Glue down the pasta shapes for the spine, ribs, pelvis, and shoulder blades.

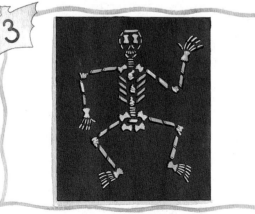

Add pasta arms, legs, hands, fingers, toes, and a skull. Use popping corn for his teeth.

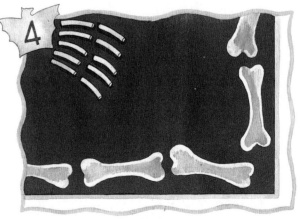

Print a border of white bones all around the edge of the poster board (see paint tip).

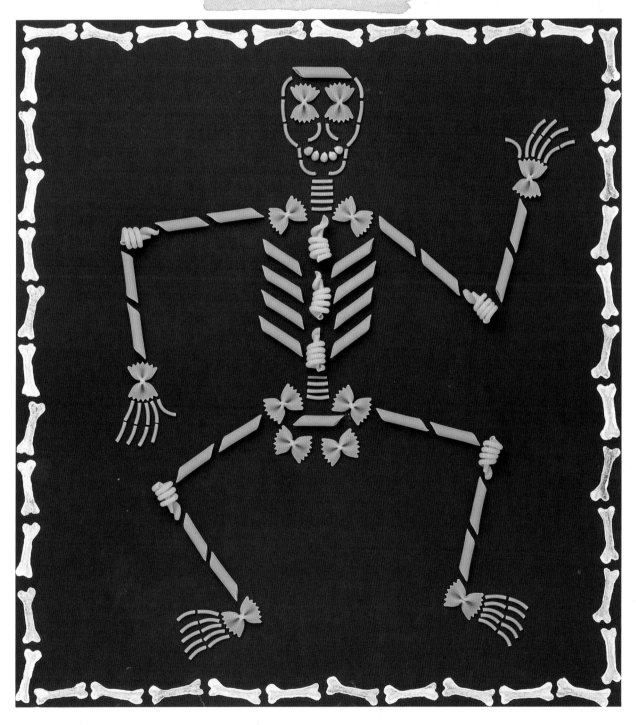

19

Spooky sky

Make a night sky picture to stick on a window, with stars, moons, and colorful paper bats. In the day, light will shine through the tissue paper and make the bats and stars really stand out. At night, the sky will turn a deep, dark blue.

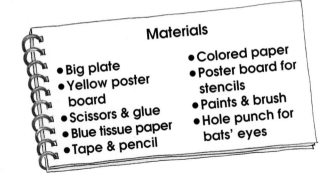

Materials
- Big plate
- Yellow poster board
- Scissors & glue
- Blue tissue paper
- Tape & pencil
- Colored paper
- Poster board for stencils
- Paints & brush
- Hole punch for bats' eyes

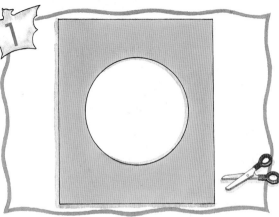

Trace a big plate in the center of the yellow poster board to make a big circle. Cut it out.

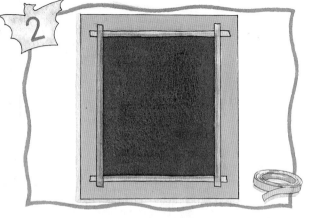

Tape a piece of dark blue tissue paper across the back of the hole.

Cut out bats and stars from colored paper. Carefully glue them onto the tissue sky.

Stencil bats, stars, and moons all around the edges of the poster board (see paint tip).

PAINT TIP
Draw each spooky shape on
a piece of board. Cut out the
inside. Press the stencil down
on the yellow poster board
and paint inside it. Gently lift
it off. Wipe off any paint
before you use it again.

A Horrible Hand

Here's a truly horrible, hairy hand picture. The easiest way to make the hand shape is to trace an adult's hand onto some paper. Make the fingers longer than they really are. Print a potato-cut border of scary, smiling skulls.

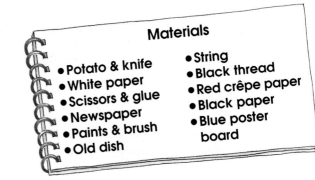

Materials

- Potato & knife
- White paper
- Scissors & glue
- Newspaper
- Paints & brush
- Old dish
- String
- Black thread
- Red crêpe paper
- Black paper
- Blue poster board

Cut out a paper hand with long fingers. Glue rolled-up newspaper on it, as shown.

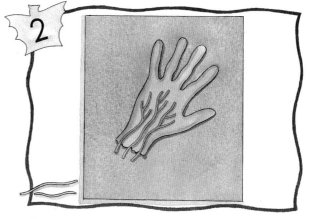

Turn the hand over and paint it. Glue it on the board. Glue on string veins painted blue.

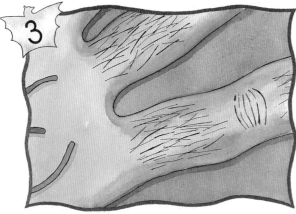

Dab glue on the wrist and fingers. Press on black thread for hair. Paint black knuckles.

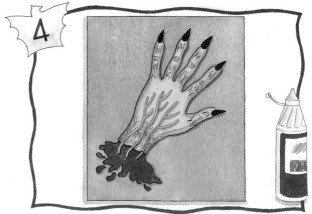

Make some blood (see paint tip). Dab it under the wrist. Add shiny black paper nails.

PAINT TIP
To make a gooey blood mixture, mix an equal amount of red paint with some glue in an old dish. Stir in some strips of red crêpe paper to make the blood look extra thick.

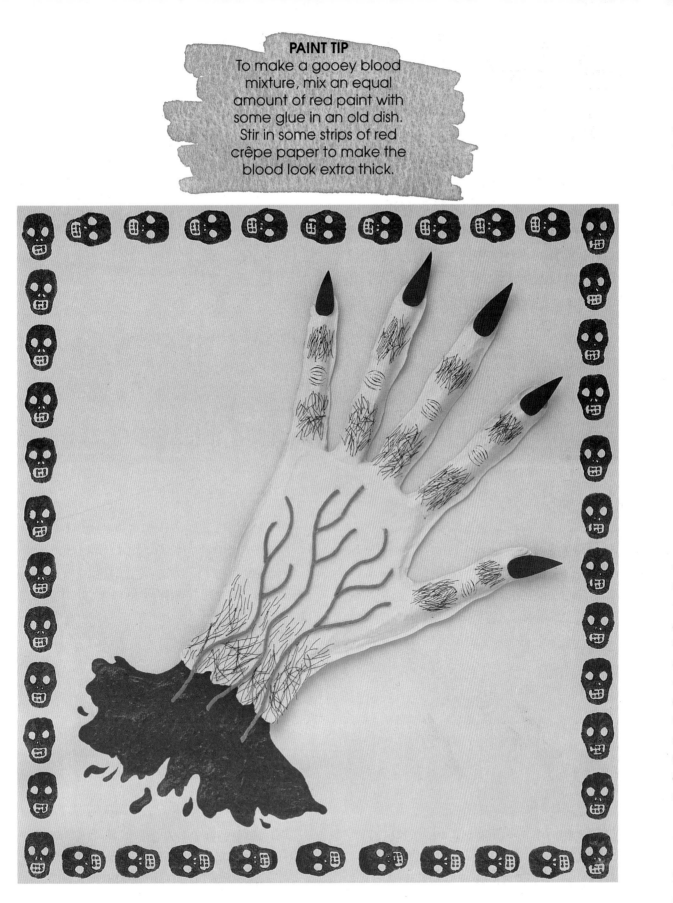

23

A Wicked Witch

Draw a big, ugly old witch with a dress, cloak, and pointed hat. Then use the outlines to cut out a poster board head, hands, and felt clothes. Give her long, straggly, sparkly hair. Let her streak across the sky on her broomstick.

Materials

- Pencil & paper
- Felt & scissors
- Striped fabric
- Paints & brush
- Glue
- Sawdust
- Twigs and string
- Purple & white poster board
- Sticky stars
- Lace & ric-rac
- Tinsel or cotton

Cut out a felt hat, cloak, and dress. Glue felt stars and moons on the dress. Cut out two legs.

Draw a witch's face and hands on white board. Cut them out and paint them (see paint tip).

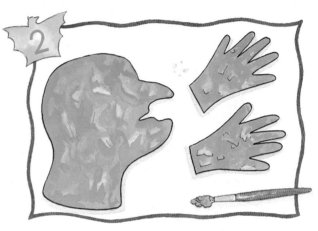

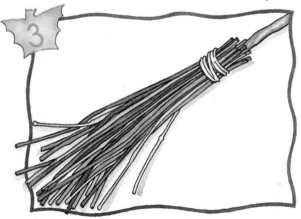

Use string to bind a bunch of thin twigs around a long stick, to make a witch's broomstick.

Glue everything on the board. Add sticky stars. Glue on a petticoat, ric-rac, and hair.

Peculiar Pumpkins

Here's a magical way of making a pumpkin picture or poster for Halloween.

Watch their grisly, grinning faces appear as you wash away the white paint.

Draw three grinning pumpkin faces on the orange board with a border of creepy shapes.

Brush white paint over the pumpkins and creepy shapes (see paint tip). Let them dry.

Materials

- Pencil
- Long sheet of orange poster board
- White paint
- Thin paintbrush
- Thick paintbrush
- Old dish
- Black India ink or waterproof ink
- Running water
- Sponge

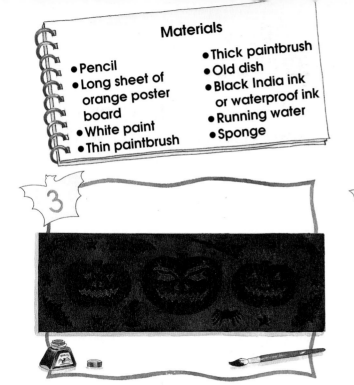

PAINT TIP
Paint a thin layer of white paint over the parts of the picture you want to keep the same color as the poster board. Use any color ink or poster board you like.

Cover the whole picture with black India ink, using a thick brush. Let the ink dry.

Hold the picture under the tap. Gently rub off the paint with a sponge. Let it dry.

27

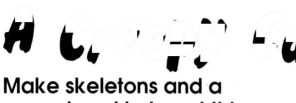

A Creepy Castle

Make skeletons and a green hand to haunt this creepy castle. Ask an adult to help you cut out the windows and a door that opens. Add a pipe cleaner chandelier, cotton ball cobwebs, and ghosts lurking behind the windows.

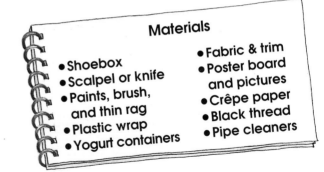

Materials

- Shoebox
- Scalpel or knife
- Paints, brush, and thin rag
- Plastic wrap
- Yogurt containers
- Fabric & trim
- Poster board and pictures
- Crêpe paper
- Black thread
- Pipe cleaners

Paint the box (see paint tip). Paint the door and cover the windows with plastic wrap.

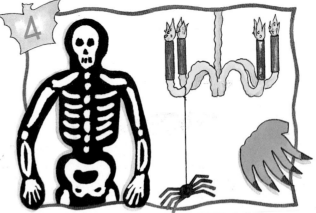

Cut pictures from magazines. Glue them on board frames. Glue the frames on the walls.

Cut a chair and stool out of yogurt containers. Glue fabric over them. Add trimmings.

Make painted crêpe skeletons, a hand, and a chandelier with a dangling spider. Glue in place.

PAINT TIP

To give the castle walls and floor a stony look, paint the inside of the box light gray. Let the paint dry. Then dip a scrunched-up thin rag into darker gray paint. Dab it over the light gray base.